The Wonder of Barbie®

Dolls and Accessories
1976 - 1986

Paris & Susan Manos

The Wonder of Barbie®

Dolls and Accessories
1976 - 1986

Paris & Susan Manos

COLLECTOR BOOKS
A Division of Schroeder Publishing Co., Inc.

The current values in this book should be used only as a guide. They are not intended to set prices, which vary from one section of the country to another. Auction prices as well as dealer prices vary greatly and are affected by condition as well as demand. Neither the Author nor the Publisher assumes responsibility for any losses that might be incurred as a result of consulting this guide.

DEDICATION

This book is dedicated in memory of Barbara Boury, a friend I never met who brought me so much joy with her Barbie finds for my collection.

Special Thanks To:

Dora Spyros
Irina Creaser
Ingelore Streng
Earika McCarthy
And above all, Mattel, Inc.

FOREWORD

"The World of Barbie" was written to help the collector.

As long as Barbie dolls are produced, the fascination for collecting this charmer and the need for more information will be endless.

"The Wonder of Barbie" features the last ten years of Barbie doll production, 1976 to 1986.

Information compiled in these pages will enable the collector to continue this quest in this intriguing hobby of collecting the most popular doll in the world.

PRICING GUIDE

Because of the short time lapse, pricing in this book is based on boxed items only.

This means never removed from the original container.

If items have been removed but never played with, they will be priced at one third (⅓) the given value. Anything beyond this is not considered collector quality.

The prices shown in this guide are derived by the authors, wholly independent of Mattel and Mattel has no connection therewith.

This book makes reference to BARBIE® and other identities for various dolls produced by Mattel, Inc. which are trademarks of Mattel.

INTRODUCTION

With our last book being such a success, and having received many re-
uests to show the recent collectible Barbie Dolls, we have decided to pro-
uce another, featuring the last ten years of the World of Barbie, 1976 to
986.

Many things have happened to the Barbie Doll during this last decade.
In 1976, Barbie helped America celebrate the Bicentennial, in her Spirit
f America dress.

Since then, Barbie has become a "Super Star". She has been endowed
ith "Quick Curl" hair. A lover of the art of dance, she became a Prima
Ballerina", a "Fashion Photo" model and received many "Pretty Changes"
ith her extra hair pieces.

She has written to many friends, and being a "Kissing" Barbie has seal-
d her letters with a kiss.

Barbie is an expert in cosmotology, and shared many "Beauty Secrets"
ith us.

Barbie has enjoyed many outdoor sports such as "Roller Skating", and
ecame a world traveler by visiting such countries as France, England, Ita-
, Scotland, The Orient, Spain, Sweden, India, Ireland, Switzerland, Japan,
nd many others.

In 1980, the Barbie Doll celebrated her twenty-first birthday. Many of
er fans were present in New York to join in on the festivities, thus
stablishing the first Barbie Doll Collectors Convention, proving to be the
eginning of something big. Since then there have been four annual con-
entions held in her honor.

Through these last few years, Barbie has become a "Golden Dream" and
uch more. Clad in her shimmering rodeo garb, she was a "Western" star
hat would wink at anyone who would give her a pat on the back.

She became the "First Barbie" little girls everywhere loved playing with.
The Barbie doll's "Magic Curl" hair was all the rage, and in her "Pink
' Pretty" gown she became the talk of the town.

But even with all her glamor, she maintained her down-to-earth qualities
y wearing her "Fashion Jeans" when she went to visit the stables because
he is a "Horse Lovin" gal.

In the evening, she went on her "Dream Date" with Ken, who loves her
Angel Face".

In 1984, the Barbie Doll celebrated her twenty-fifth (silver) Anniversary
y attending a gala in her "Crystal" gown. This was the year she let
veryone know how much she was "Lovin' You" by teaching us how to
xercise and have a "Great Shape".

Barbie has little "Dreamtime" because being such a YUPPIE, she works "Day-to-Night" with just enough time to attend the "Peaches n' Cream" Ball.

This year, 1986, Barbie is going to visit other countries including the "Tropical" regions and Greece and Peru.

In the evening the Barbie Doll will wear her "Dream Glow" gown and travel as "Astronaut" with "The Rockers", her musical group.

Truly, Barbie has made some unbelievable "Magic Moves" with her "Gift Giving" ways.

Through this introduction, you have been given a glimpse of what has happened to the world's favorite doll during the past ten years.

Now as you leaf through the following pages you will see for yourself.

Paris and I wish you many moments of pleasure in your quest for these Barbie Doll treasures.

TABLE OF CONTENTS

A NOTE TO THE FUTURE COLLECTOR

Barbie Dolls are highly collectible and anyone, man, woman or child ca collect them.

In our case it is all three of us. Our daughter Carol, now twenty-one, bega playing with Barbie at the age of four. When she grew too old to play wit dolls, she started collecting them.

As time went by, having collected antique dolls for years, I became in terested in this little lady of fashion and began collecting Barbie Dolls alon with Carol.

Through these years Barbie has been the bridge between the generatior for Carol and me. I must say Barbie was about the only thing Carol an I had in common during her early teen years.

By the time Carol turned sixteen, Paris started showing an interest i this little goodwill ambassador. Not as a plaything, but as an investmen And because Barbie is so photogenic, a new interest in the hobby o photography resulted from it.

With the help of Carol's knowledge of Barbie, my experience in apprai ing, mixed with Paris's love of photography, we, as a family, authored ou first Barbie picture price guide. This goes to show where Barbie Doll cc lecting can lead.

What I am trying to convey to the new collector is the fact that you d not have to be wealthy to enjoy this hobby.

Barbie is one of the most collectible items on the market, today.

Just start off with the International Barbie Dolls sold in Departmer Stores or the dark skinned Barbie Dolls.

There still are many earlier Barbie Dolls to be found out there.

Individually owned toy stores with old stock, or small five and dime o hardware stores are ideal places to find dolls dating as far back as 198o

Before you know it, you have made a small investment in pleasure, wit interest-paying results.

Happy Collecting,

Susan Manos

Ten Years Of Barbie
1976-1986

1976 "Free Moving Barbie" Cara & P.J., $35.00 M.I.B.

1976 "Free Moving Ken", $35.00 M.I.B. 1976 "Free Moving Curtis." Curtis sold for a brief time and only as a Free Moving. $50.00 M.I.B.

1976 "Gold Medal Barbie" U.S. Olympics, $30.00 M.I.B. 1976 "Gold Medal Barbie" Skater, $45.00 M.I.B.

1976 "Gold Medal Barbie" Skier, $45.00 M.I.B. 1976 "Gold Medal Ken" Skier, $45.00 M.I.B.

1976 "Quick Curl Miss America" signed by designer, $35.00 M.I.B.

1976 "The Now Look Ken", $30.00 M.I.B.

1976 "Growing Up Skipper", $22.00 M.I.B.

1976 "Beautiful Bride Barbie" sold only in department stores, $60.00 M.I.B.

14

1976 "Ballerina Barbie", $30.00 M.I.B.

1976 "Ballerina Cara", $35.00 M.I.B.

1976 "Deluxe Quick Curl Barbie" with Jergens children's toiletries, $35.00 M.I.B
1976 "Deluxe Quick Curl Barbie" from Canada, $30.00 M.I.B.

1976 "Deluxe Quick Curl P.J.", $30.00 M.I.B. 1976 "Deluxe Quick Curl Cara", $35.0•
M.I.B.

1976 "Barbie Super Fashion Fireworks" sold in selected stores only, $45.00 M.I.P.

1976 "Barbie Super Fashion Fireworks" sold in selected stores, $45.00 M.I.P.

1976 "Barbie Super Fashion Fireworks" sold in selected stores only, $45.00 M.I.P.

1976 "Barbie Plus 3" sold in selected stores only, $45.00 M.I.P.

1977 "Super Star Barbie" with free gift, two variations, $60.00 M.I.B.

1977 "Super Star Ken" with free gift, $60.00 M.I.B. 1977 "Super Star Barbie & Ken Set" department store special. Hard to find. $100.00 M.I.B.

1977 "Super Star Barbie" with free gift, $55.00 M.I.B. "Super Star Barbie", $50.00 M.I.B. "Super Star Christie", $50.00 M.I.B.

1977 "Super Size Barbie", $30.00 M.I.B. "Super Size Christie", $35.00 M.I.B.

1977 "Growing Up Ginger", Skipper's friend - sold for a brief time, $25.00 M.I.B.

1977 "Hawaiian Super Star Barbie" from Canada - hard to find. $50.00 M.I.B.

1978 "Fashion Photo Barbie", two variations, $30.00 M.I.B.

1978 "Fashion Photo Christie", "Fashion Photo P.J.", $30.00 M.I.B.

1978 "Super Star Barbie", "In The Spotlight", $60.00 M.I.B. 1978 "Super Star Barbie", "Fashion Change-Abouts", $45.00 M.I.B.

1978 "Beautiful Bride Barbie", $25.00 M.I.B.

1978 "Malibu Francis, Skipper, P.J., Barbie, Christie, Ken", $15.00 M.I.B.

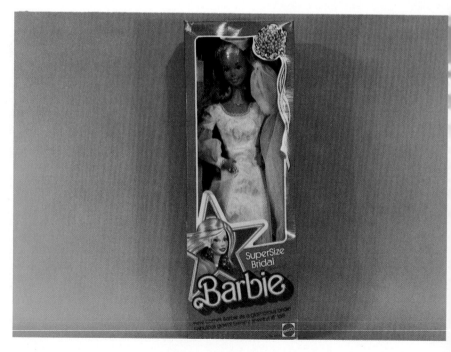

1978 "Super Size Bridal Barbie" sold for a brief time. $40.00 M.I.B.

1978 "Malibu Barbie" Fashion Combo sold in select stores, $25.00 M.I.B.

1979 "Kissing Barbie" department store special. Comes with extra dress. $40.00 M.I.B.

1979 "Kissing Christie", $30.00 M.I.B. Kissing Barbie, two hair style variations. Parted Style, $30.00; Bangs Style, $40.00 M.I.B.

1979 "Pretty Changes Barbie", $25.00 M.I.B. With free gift offer, $30.00 M.I.B.

1979 "Pretty Changes Barbie" Lamp sold in discount stores. Doll and lamp base boxed together. $40.00

1979 "Ballerina Barbie On Tour" sold at selected stores, $35.00 M.I.B. "Ballerina Barbie", $25.00 M.I.B.

1979 "Super Teen Skipper", $18.00 M.I.B.

1979 "Sun Lovin' Malibu P.J., Christie, Skipper, Barbie & Ken", $12.00 M.I.B.

1979 "Super Size Barbie with Super Hair." Last of the large size dolls, $30.00.

1980 "Beauty Secrets Barbie", "Beauty Secrets Christie", $15.00 M.I.B.

1980 "Beauty Secrets Barbie Pretty Reflections" gift set sold only in department stores. 1 year only. $35.00

1980 "Black Barbie" came in many hair style variations. $15.00 M.I.B.

1980 "Roller Skating Barbie", $18.00 M.I.B. "Roller Skating Ken", $18.00 M.I.B.

1980 "Scott", Skipper's boyfriend sold for a brief time. $20.00 M.I.B.

1980 "Sport & Shave Ken", sold for brief time. $18.00 M.I.B.

1980 "Hispanic Barbie", sold mostly in special areas, $20.00 M.I.B.

1980 "Italian Barbie", one of the first three from the International Series. Department store specials, $45.00 M.I.B.

1980 "Parisian Barbie", one of the first three from the International Series. Department store specials, $45.00 M.I.B.

1980 "Royal Barbie", another of the first three Barbies from the International Series. Department store specials, $45.00 M.I.B.

1981 "Golden Dream Barbie." First issue came with unusual hair style. Later issue came in long soft style. In some cases heads were changed at stores. The extra heads were discarded. Unusual style, $35.00 M.I.B.; Regular style, $20.00 M.I.B.; Extra heads, $5.00.

1980 "Golden Dream Christie", second issue, $20.00 M.I.B.; First issue (note variation in box and gloves), $25.00. M.I.B. "Golden Dream Barbie". Department store special. One year only. $40.00 M.I.B.

1981 "Western Barbie", $15.00 M.I.B. "Western Skipper", $15.00 M.I.B. "Western Ken", $15.00 M.I.B.

1980 "My First Barbie", first time on the market. $18.00 M.I.B.

1981 "Happy Birthday Barbie", $18.00 M.I.B.

1981 "Scottish Barbie", second set from the International Series. Department store special. $40.00 M.I.B. 1981 "Oriental Barbie", second set from the International Series. Department store special. $40.00 M.I.B.

1982 "Pink & Pretty Christie", $25.00 M.I.B. "Pink & Pretty Barbie", $25.00 M.I.B.

1982 "Pink & Pretty Barbie." Note different fabric bodice, signed by designer. Not priced. "Pink & Pretty Barbie." Extra special gift set sold in department stores. One year only. $35.00 M.I.B.

1982 "Magic Curl Barbie", white & black. $20.00 M.I.B.

1982 "Fashion Jeans Ken", $19.00 M.I.B. "Fashion Jeans Barbie", $19.00 M.I.B.

1982 "All Star Ken", $18.00 M.I.B.

1982 "Sunsational Malibu Ken, Barbie, P.J., Skipper, Christie & Black Ken", $15.00 each.

"Hawaiian Barbie", sold in department stores only. Two variations. $25.00 each.

1982 "Eskimo Barbie", one of Third Set from the International Series. Department store special. $40.00 M.I.B. "India Barbie", another of the Third Set from the International Series. Department store special. $40.00 M.I.B.

1983 "Dream Date P.J.", "Dream Date Ken", "Dream Date Barbie", $18.00 each.

1983 "Tracy & Todd Bridal Pair", $15.00 each.

1983 "Twirly Curls Barbie", White, Black, Hispanic. $15.00 each.

983 "Twirly Curls Barbie", gift set. Department store special. One year only. $45.00
.I.B.

983 "Angel Face Barbie", $15.00 M.I.B. 1983 "My First Barbie", second issue,
15.00 M.I.B.

1983 "Happy Birthday Barbie", second issue, $15.00 M.I.B. 1983 "Ballerina Barbie", sold at Mervyn's Department Store only. $18.00 M.I.B.

1983 "Horse Lovin Barbie", "Horse Lovin Skipper", "Horse Lovin Ken", sold f brief time. Barbie, $25.00 M.I.B. Skipper, $20.00 M.I.B. Ken, $25.00 M.I.B.

1983 "Barbie & Ken Campin' Out Set", sold at selected stores out West. $65.00
M.I.B.

1983 "Barbie & Friends". Three dolls packaged in one box. Still available in stores,
at $25.00.

1983 "Spanish Barbie". One of the Fourth Set from the International Series. Depart
ment store special. $35.00 M.I.B. 1983 "Swedish Barbie". One of the Fourth Set
from the International Series. Department store special. $35.00 M.I.B.

1984 "Crystal Ken", "Crystal Barbie", "Crystal Black Barbie", $15.00; "Crystal
Black Ken", hard to find. $20.00 M.I.B.

1984 "Happy Birthday Barbie", third issue. $15.00 M.I.B.

1984 "Sweet Roses P.J.", $15.00 M.I.B. 1984 "Loving You Barbie", $15.00 M.I.B.

1984 "Loving You Barbie", gift set sold only in department stores. One year only.
$45.00.

1984 "Sun Gold Malibu Barbie, P.J., Black Barbie, Skipper, Ken, Black Ken", still available.

1984 "Sunsational Black Ken, Hispanic Barbie, Hispanic Ken", $10.00 each M.I.B.

1984 "Great Shape Barbie, Skipper & Ken", $15.00 each. These dolls are different than the 1986 issue.

1984 "Swiss Barbie", "Irish Barbie", fifth issue of the International Series. Department Store special. Still available.

1985 "Day-To-Night Hispanic Barbie", only sold in selected areas. $15.00 M.I.B. Other "Day-To-Night" Barbie Dolls still available.

1985 "Day-To-Night Black Ken and White Ken", still available.

1985 "Peaches 'n Cream Barbie". Still available.

1985 "My First Barbie", third issue. Two different hair styles. One has old style, the other has bangs. Old hair style, $12.00 M.I.B. Others, still available.

1985 "Dreamtime Barbie", still available. 1985 "Hot Stuff Skipper", still available.

1985 "Dance Sensation Barbie" gift set sold at selected stores only. $18.00 M.I.B.

1985 "Happy Birthday Barbie" gift set, department store special. One year only. $25.00 M.I.B.

1985 "Japanese Barbie", sixth issue of the International Series. Department store special. Still available.

1986 "Dream Glow Barbie", "Dream Glow Ken" Black Set. These dolls are valued at today's market price.

1986 "Dream Glow Barbie", "Dream Glow Ken" White Set. These dolls are valued at today's market price.

1986 "Barbie Rockers", friend Dana & Dee Dee. Valued at today's market price.

1986 "Barbie Rockers", Derek & Diva. These dolls are valued at today's market price.

1986 "Barbie Rockers". Two boxed variations. This is the reason why dolls should remain Mint-in-box.

1986 "Gift Giving Barbie". This doll is valued at today's market price. Here is another reason why Mint-in-box is stressed for collectibility. Once the box has been opened, the little items get misplaced.

1986 "Tropical Barbie", "Tropical Skipper", and "Tropical Ken". These dolls are valued at today's market price.

1986 "Tropical Barbie", "Tropical Ken" Black Set. "Tropical Miko", Barbie's new friend. These dolls are valued at today's market price.

1986 "Astronaut Barbie". At the time of constructing this book this doll had not appeared on the market. No price as yet. Photo, courtesy of Mattel, © Mattel, Inc. 1986.

1986 "Magic Moves Barbie". At the time of printing this doll had not been released on the market. Not priced yet. Photo courtesy of Mattel, © Mattel, Inc. 1986.

Barbie Doll Family Dolls

"Marie Osmond", $15.00 M.I.B. "Donny Osmond", $15.00 M.I.B.

"Jimmy Osmond", sold in Canada, $25.00 M.I.B. "Donny and Marie Osmond Gift Set", $40.00 M.I.B.

"Debby Boone Doll", $25.00 M.I.B. "Kristie McNichol" as Buddy from the TV show "Family." $25.00 M.I.B. "Kitty O'Neil", well-known racer. $25.00 M.I.B.

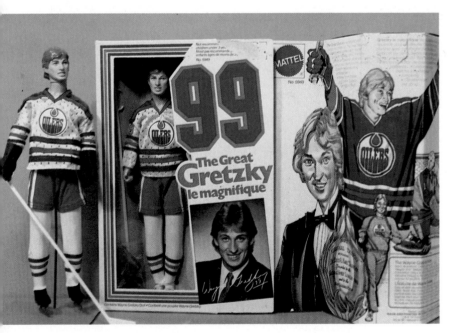

"Wayne Gretzky", famous Hockey Player for the Edmonton Oilers. This doll was made to be sold in Canada, but a few did filter through to the States. $30.00 M.I.B.

"Chantal Goya", well-known singer in France. Sold in Europe. $85.00 M.I.B.

Extra outfits were made for "Chantal Goya". Some came in boxes marked "Barbie & Chantal Goya". Others came in boxes bearing her name only. The latter are valued more. $25.00 to $30.00 M.I.B.

"Guardian Goddesses", "Sun Spell and Moon Mystic". These dolls were sold in a few selected areas. They were made as a tryout doll. $75.00 each M.I.B.

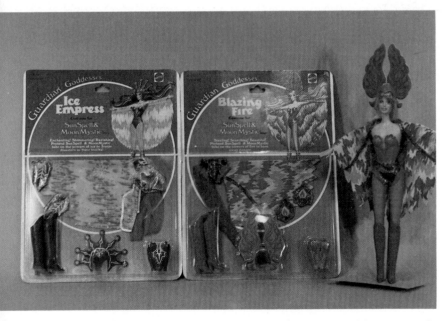

"Ice Empress" and "Blazing Fire" Outfits. Sold where dolls were sold. $25.00 each M.I.P.

"Lion Queen", "Soaring Eagle", sold where dolls were sold. $35.00 each M.I.P.

"Rare Francie" sold only in Germany. Note catalogue page. Very hard to find. $200.00 M.I.P.

Barbie Dolls From Europe and Canada

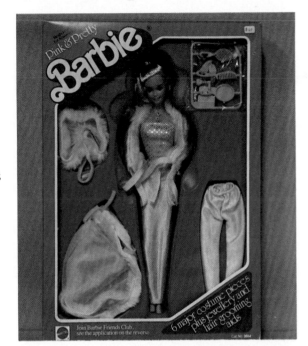

"Pink & Pretty Barbie" gift set from England, $75.00.

"Snow Princess Dog Sled" from Sweden, $100.00 M.I.B. "Snow Princess Barbie" from Sweden, $150.00 M.I.B.

"Pretty Changes Barbie" and "Beauty" Barbie's dog. Packaged together in a gift set. Sold in France, $100.00 M.I.B.

"Safari Ken", "Safari Skipper", "Safari Barbie". Sold in some European Countries, $45.00 each M.I.B.

"Super Sport Ken" from Canada, $20.00 M.I.B. "Super Dance Skipper" from Germany, $40.00 M.I.B. "Super Dance Barbie" from Canada, $20.00 M.I.B.

"Sea Lovin Ken" from Europe, $35.00. "Sea Lovin Skipper" from Europe, $35.00. "Sea Lovin Barbie" from Canada, $25.00 M.I.B.

"Golden Nights Barbie" from Canada, $35.00. "Disco Skipper" from Germany, $40.00. "Golden Nights Ken" from Canada, $35.00.

"Jeans Barbie", "Jeans Skipper", and "Jeans Ken" from Europe, $30.00 M.I.B.

"California Barbie", "Trinidad Barbie" from Italy, $35.00 each M.I.B.

"Fashion Fantasy" outfit sold in U.S., $8.00 M.I.P. "Partytime Barbie" sold in Canada, $25.00.

"Picture Pretty Barbie" from Canada, $25.00 M.I.B.

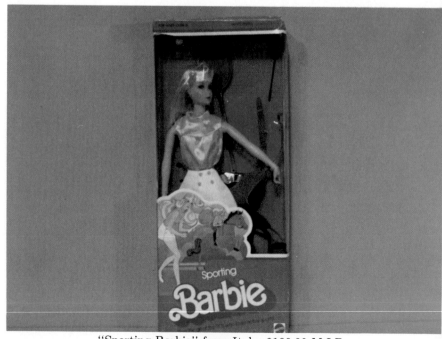

"Sporting Barbie" from Italy, $100.00 M.I.B.

"Fashion Play Barbie" dressed in Quick Curl Cara dress. From Germany, $35.00 M.I.B. 1985 "Ballerina Barbie" from Germany, $35.00 M.I.B.

"Fashion Barbies" from Europe and Canada, $18.00 each M.I.B.

"Fashion Play Barbie" from Canada, $18.00 each M.I.B.

"Valerie Tahitiana" made from Barbie head mold. From Mexico, $125.00 M.I.B.
"Barbie Hawaiana" from Mexico, $125.00 M.I.B.

Equestrienne Barbie", two different facial features. From Germany, $45.00 M.I.B.

"My First Barbie" from Germany, $45.00 M.I.B. "My First Barbie" from England, $50.00 M.I.B. "My First Barbie" promo with extra outfit, from Germany, $40.00 M.I.B.

"Barbie Sun" from Spain, $45.00 M.I.B. "Barbie Super Star" from Spain, $55.0 M.I.B.

"Muñeca Barbie" from Spain, $55.00 M.I.B. "Beauty Secrets Barbie" from Spai $45.00 M.I.B.

"Fabulous Fur Barbie" from Canada, $35.00. "Fabulous Fur Barbie" from Germany, $35.00.

"Partytime Barbie" from Canada, $25.00 M.I.B. "Partytime Barbie" from Europe, $35.00 M.I.B. "Pretty Party Barbie" from Canada, $20.00 M.I.B.

"Quick Curl Cara" from Canada, $35.00 M.I.B.

"Inexpensive Fashion Barbie" from Europe and Canada, $12.00 each M.I.B.

"Barbie St. Trop" from France, $50.00 M.I.B. "Simpatia Barbie" from Italy, $35.00 M.I.B. "Fashion Barbie" from Canada, $15.00 M.I.B.

"Springtime Magic Outfit" sold in U.S.A., $20.00 M.I.B. Sold on Barbie in Germany, $35.00 M.I.B.

"Barbie Roller Gift Set" from Spain, $65.00.

"Western Barbie" from Spain, $65.00 M.I.B.

すてきな バービー
ローズパル

♪ランランラ ラッタッタ！
ヘルメットをかぶったバービーの
おかいものファッション！

フルーツショップ

車(イタリー製)・バ　　人形(ヘルメットつき)・ワ　　　　　　―ヘルメットをかぶりましょう―

"Barbie Gift Set" with Skooter and Dressed Doll. From Japan, $175.00.

MATTEL

NOT RECOMMENDED
FOR CHILDREN UNDER 3
NON RECOMMANDÉ AUX
ENFANTS DE MOINS DE 3 ANS

Barbie

Barbie

美しい装い●
輝くダイヤモンドアクセサリー●
いろいろできるポーズがたのしめます●

すてきな・・・
バービー

●イヤリング●ネックレス●指輪
●シューズ●スタンド付

Dressed Doll" from Canada, $15.00 M.I.P. "Super Star Barbie" from Japan, $75.00
M.I.B.

"Dressed Doll" from Canada, $15.00 M.I.P. "Super Star Barbie" from Japan, $75.00 M.I.B.

"Dressed Doll" from Canada, $15.00 M.I.P. "Beautiful Bride Barbie" from Japan, $75.00.

"Dressed Doll" from Canada, $15.00 M.I.P. "Super Star Barbie" from Japan, $75.00 M.I.B.

This group of Barbie dolls is dressed in outfits made for earlier dolls. Sold in Canada, $15.00 each M.I.B.

The following group of Barbie dolls is dressed in outfits made for earlier dolls. Sold in Canada, $15.00 each M.I.B.

Barbie Dolls From Japan

The group of Barbie Dolls in this chapter was made in Japan by the Takara Toy Company. Takara had been licensed by Mattel to use the name Barbie for their dolls. This Amerasian Barbie looks quite different than the other Barbie Dolls. They have been accepted favorably by the collector and considered highly collectible.

"Dress Kimono Barbie" Japanese Traditional Style. Light summer colors. $75.00 each.

"Dream Barbie Dress Kimono Barbie", darker colors, $75.00 each M.I.B.

"Everyday Kimono Dolls", $70.00 each M.I.B. Extra Kimono Set, $45.00 M.I.B.

"Dress Collection Dress Kimonos", $50.00 each M.I.B.

"Dream Barbie" Red Gown, $75.00; Pink Evening Dress, $75.00; Pink Party Dress, $70.00.

"City Colors" set of six Barbies priced as complete set, $400.00; individually, $60.00 each.

"Dream Barbie" Evening Dress, $75.00 M.I.B. Dress Pant Suit, $70.00 M.I.B. "Crystal Barbie" Party Dress $75.00, Gown $80.00.

"White Fantasy Barbie", $75.00 each M.I.B.

"Sweet Country Barbie" dressed in summer clothes, $70.00 each M.I.B. Dressed in Fall clothes, $75.00 M.I.B.

"Sweet Kiss Barbie". This Barbie came with extra accessories and a Barbie wrist tag. $85.00 each M.I.B.

90

"Excelina Barbie", extra special quality, $80.00 each.

"Casual Barbie" Baseball Outfit, $60.00, M.I.B. "Sweet Pop Barbie" with extra accessories, $85.00 M.I.B. "Sweet Pop Barbie", $70.00 M.I.B.

"Ellie", Barbie's friend. $70.00 each M.I.B. "Flora", Barbie's friend. $70.00 each M.I.B.

"Wedding Barbie", $80.00 each M.I.B.

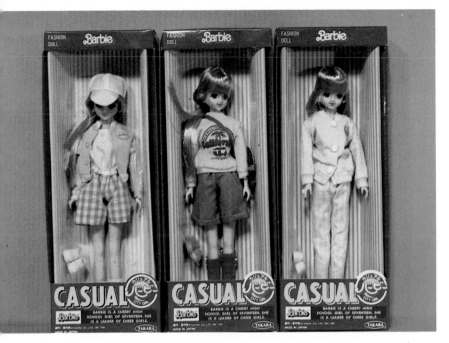

"Casual Barbie" Play Outfits, $50.00 each M.I.B.

"Fashion Barbie" inexpensive line, $50.00 each M.I.B.

"Romantic Barbie", most expensive of the line. $125.00 M.I.B.

"Fur Collection Gift Set", $65.00 M.I.B.

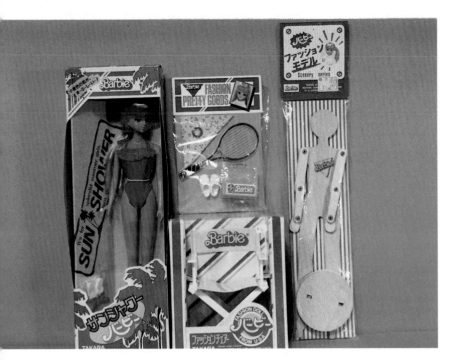

"Sun Shower Barbie" limited offer, $65.00 M.I.B. "Play Set", $15.00 M.I.P. "Directors Chair", $20.00 M.I.B. "Wooden Mannequin", $15.00 M.I.P.

"Ken", Barbie's Boy Friend. Dress Suits, $75.00 each M.I.B. Casual Clothes, $70.00 each M.I.B.

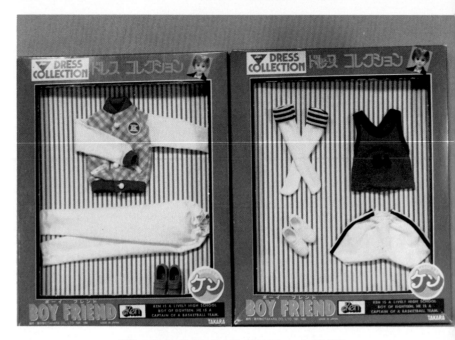

"Ken Suit Collection", $25.00 each M.I.B.

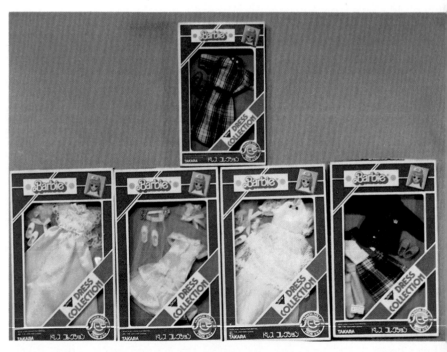

"Barbie Dress Collection", Top, $20.00 M.I.B. Bottom, $30.00 each M.I.B.

Paper Dolls 1976-1986

Boxed Paper Dolls. "Western Skipper", $10.00 uncut; "Western Barbie", $10.00 uncut; "Golden Dream Barbie", $12.00 uncut.

Boxed Paper Dolls. "Malibu Barbie", "Pink & Pretty Barbie", "Angel Face Barbie", $10.00 each uncut.

Boxed Paper Dolls. "Super Star Barbie", $15.00 uncut; "Fashion Photo Barbie", $15.00 uncut; "Kissing Barbie", $12.00 uncut.

Boxed Paper Dolls. "Quick Curl Barbie", $15.00 uncut; "Pretty Changes", $15.00 uncut; "Super Teen, Skipper & Scott", $15.00 uncut.

"Fantasy Barbie", $4.00 uncut; "Christmas Time", Limited Edition, $15.00 uncut.

"Day-To-Night", "Peaches n' Cream", still available.

"Crystal Barbie", "Twirly Curls Barbie", $4.00 each uncut.

"Great Shape Barbie", "Barbie & Ken", still available.

"Sunsational Barbie", $3.00 uncut; "Pink & Pretty" Paper Doll & Playbook, $10.00 uncut.

"Western Barbie", $6.00 uncut; "Golden Dream", $6.00 uncut.

"Pretty Changes", $8.00 uncut; "Barbie & Skipper" Paper Doll & Play Book, $7.00 uncut.

"Angel Face", $4.00 uncut; "Jeans Barbie" Poster Book, $3.00.

Boxed "Ballerina Barbie", $6.00 uncut; "Pink & Pretty", $7.00 uncut.

"Growing Up Skipper", $7.00 uncut, "Barbie's Beach Bus", $6.00 uncut.

"Barbie Fashion Originals", $10.00 uncut; "Barbie & Her Friends", $6.00 uncut.

"Barbie Story Diary", $5.00; "Barbie Press-out Play Book", still available.

Barbie's Olympic Ski Village, $25.00 M.I.B.

"Barbie & P.J." Olympic Gymnast Set, $25.00 M.I.B.

Barbie Playhouse from Europe, $60.00 M.I.B.

Barbie Baby-Sitting Room from Canada, $60.00 M.I.B.

Me & Barbie "Birthday Party", department store special, $60.00 M.I.B.

Barbie Motor Roller (with funtime Barbie), $95.00 M.I.B.

Barbie Superstar Stage, $30.00 M.I.B.

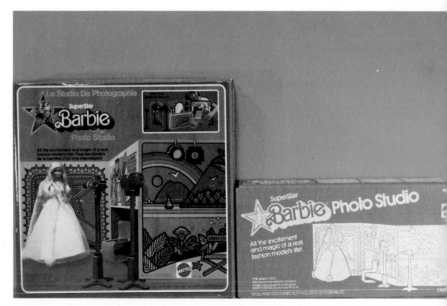

Superstar Barbie Photo Studio. From Canada, $50.00 M.I.B. Superstar Barbie Phot
Studio. Sears special, $25.00 M.I.B.

Barbie Loves McDonalds Play Shop. Still available.

"Barbie, Skipper & Ken" McDonald outfits, $20.00 each M.I.P.

Ballerina Barbie Stage, $30.00 M.I.B.

Ballerina Barbie Fashion "Snow Fairy", $25.00 M.I.B.

Ballerina Barbie Fashion "Sugar Plum Fairy". From the Nutcracker, $25.00 M.I.B.

Ballerina Barbie Fashion "Princess Aurora", from the Nutcracker, $25.00 M.I.B.

Heavenly Holidays. Collector Series I, $20.00 M.I.B. Springtime Magic. Collector
Series II, $20.00 M.I.B.

View from back of box.

Silver Sensation. Collector Series III, $25.00 M.I.B.

Oscar De La Renta. Collector Series IV-V, $15.00 each M.I.B.

Oscar De La Renta. Collector Series VI-VII, $15.00 M.I.B.

Barbie Fur Collection. From France, $30.00 each M.I.B.

Barbie Fur & Leather Collection. From Germany, $40.00 each.

Barbie Fur & Leather Collection. From Germany, $40.00 each M.I.B.

Barbie Fur & Leather Collection. From Germany, $40.00 each M.I.B.

Barbie Star Cycle, $15.00 M.I.B. Barbie Motor Bike, still available.

"Malibu Barbie" Beach Party Play Set with doll. Department store special, $40.00 M.I.Case.

Barbie Water Sports Fashion Playset. Barbie Bath Fun Fashion Playset, both still available.

Barbie Vet Fun Playset. Barbie Travel Fashion Playset, both still available.

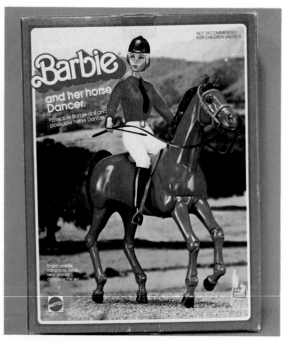

Barbie and her horse "Dancer" with Doll & Horse. Sold in Canada, $60.00 M.I.B.

"Dallas", Barbie's Horse, $15.00. Barbie's horse "Dallas". From Germany. This horse is fully jointed. $50.00 M.I.B.

"Honey", Skipper's horse, $15.00 M.I.B. "Midnight", Barbie's stallion, $15.00 M.I.B.

Barbie Travelin' Trailer, $35.00 M.I.B.

Barbie Baby-sits. From Canada, $25.00 M.I.B. Barbie Baby-sits. Sears exclusive, $20.00 M.I.B.

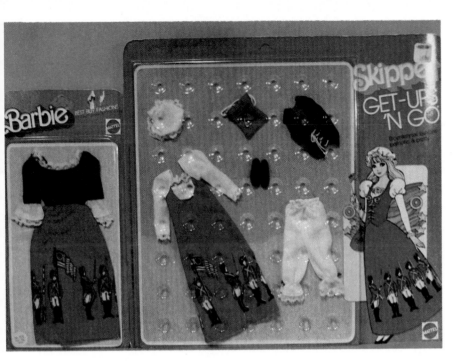

Barbie Bicentennial Dress, $25.00 M.I.P. Skipper Bicentennial Set, $30.00 M.I.P.

Barbie Silver Vette, $20.00 M.I.B.

Convention Souvenirs

1980 "First Barbie Doll Collectors Convention" held in New York. Gold Charm, Doll, Book & Badge. Limited to 150. $300.00.

1982 Second Barbie Doll Collectors Convention. Held in Michigan. Doll, Silver Charm & Book. Limited to 250. $250.00.

1983 Phoenix, Arizona Barbie Doll Collectors Convention. Limited to 250. Indian Doll, Book, Prairie Doll, & Button. Limited to 250. $300.00.

1984 Barbie Doll Collectors Convention in New York. Book, Silver Charm, Doll & Button. Limited to 250. $300.00. Cup not included.

1985 Barbie Doll Collectors Convention in Detroit, Michigan. Japanese Doll, Book, Pen & Takara Barbie. Limited to 250. $300.00.

Oddities and Rarities

Bild Lilli Dolls from Germany. Pre-Barbie Era. Small Lilli, $450.00 and up. Large Lilli, $750.00 and up.

Barbie Picnic Fishing Basket. Never issued. One of a kind. Prototype. Not Priced.

First Barbie issued (#1) $1,500.00 and up M.I.B.

Prototype Barbie. Never issued. (Is hard to find). Display Dressed Boxed Doll. Not priced.

Side view of Prototype Barbie. (One of a kind). Never issued. Not priced.

Front view of blond Prototype.

Prototype Barbie (one hole only) with reddish brown hair. (One of a kind). Never issued. Not priced.

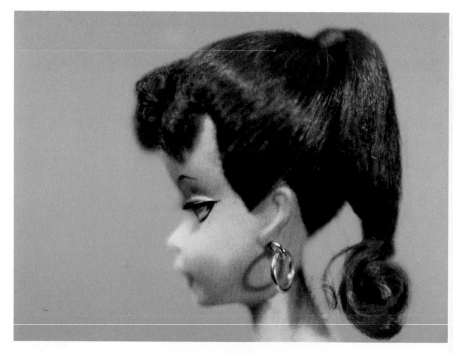

Side view of dark haired Prototype.

Unusual Gift Set with Standard Barbie. For the Inland Steel Container Company, Chicago, Illinois. Not priced.

Gift Set. Box Lid View.

Original Blond Western Barbie. Shown with rare red-headed Barbie. Not priced. Courtesy, Earika McCarthy.

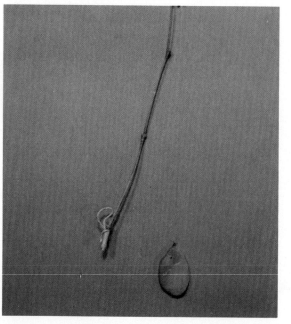

Barbie's First Fish. Made of wax. No wonder we don't see many of these around. Not priced. Courtesy, Earika McCarthy.

1981 Mattel Toy Catalogs not sent to the general public. Important Collectors Item. Not priced.

1982 Mattel Toy Catalog not sent to the general public. Very collectible. Not priced.

1983 Mattel Toy Catalog not sent to general public. At times, the merchants will give them to a collector.

Important 1984 Mattel Toy Catalog. This one is marked "Barbie Doll's 25th Anniversary." This is one that should be in collections. Not priced.

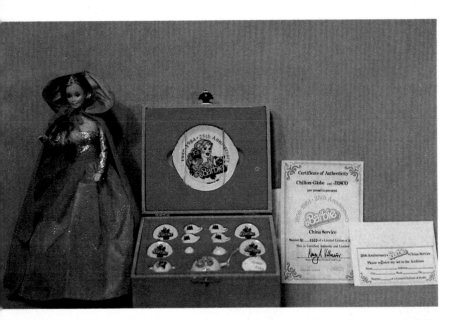

Barbie's 25th Anniversary Commemorative Items Tea Set. Limited Edition. $75.00.

25th Anniversary Champagne Glass. Special invitations and folder. Not priced.

Schroeder's Antiques Price Guide

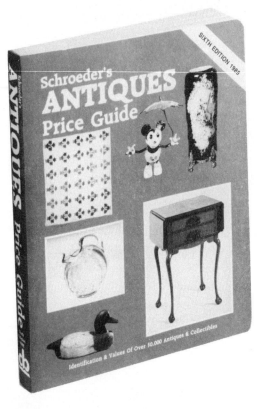

Schroeder's Antiques Price Guide has climbed its way to the top in a field already supplied with several well-established publications! The word is out, *Schroeder's Price Guide* is the best buy at any price. Over 500 categories are covered, with more than 50,000 listings. From ABC Plates to Zsolnay, if it merits the interest of today's collector, you'll find it in Schroeder's. Each subject is represented with histories and background information. In addition, hundreds of sharp original photos are used each year to illustrate not only the rare and the unusual, but the everyday "fun-type" collectibles as well. All new copy and all new illustrations make Schroeder's THE price guide on antiques and collectibles. We have not and will not simply change prices in each new edition.

The writing and researching team is backed by a staff of more than seventy of Collector Books' finest authors, as well as a board of advisors made up of well-known antique authorities and the country's top dealers, all specialists in their fields. Prices are gathered over the entire year previous to publication, then each category is thoroughly checked. Only the best of the lot remains for publication. You'll find the new edition of *Schroeder's Antiques Price Guide* the one to buy for factual information and quality.

No dealer, collector or investor can afford not to own this book. It is available from your favorite bookseller or antiques dealer at the low price of $11.95. If you are unable to find this price guide in your area, it's available from Collector Books, P.O. Box 3009, Paducah, KY 42001 at $11.95 plus $1.00 for postage and handling.